# I Love
# Spiders

**By Steve Parker**
**Illustrated by Richard Draper**

Miles Kelly

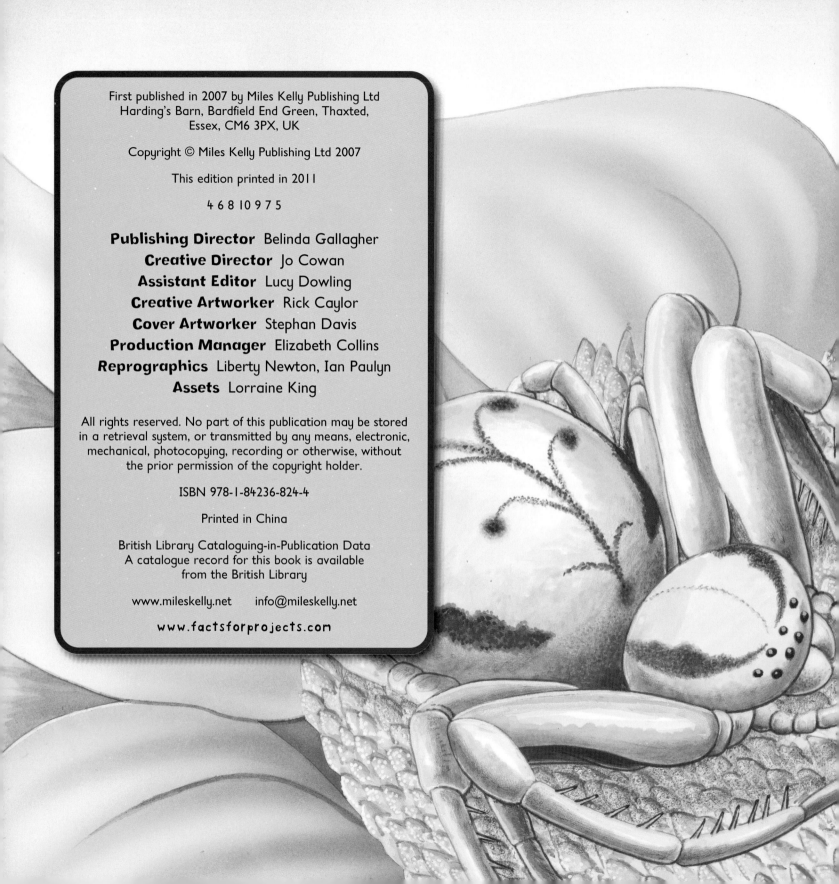

First published in 2007 by Miles Kelly Publishing Ltd
Harding's Barn, Bardfield End Green, Thaxted,
Essex, CM6 3PX, UK

Copyright © Miles Kelly Publishing Ltd 2007

This edition printed in 2011

4 6 8 10 9 7 5

**Publishing Director** Belinda Gallagher
**Creative Director** Jo Cowan
**Assistant Editor** Lucy Dowling
**Creative Artworker** Rick Caylor
**Cover Artworker** Stephan Davis
**Production Manager** Elizabeth Collins
**Reprographics** Liberty Newton, Ian Paulyn
**Assets** Lorraine King

ISBN 978-1-84236-824-4

Printed in China

British Library Cataloguing-in-Publication Data
A catalogue record for this book is available
from the British Library

www.mileskelly.net    info@mileskelly.net

www.factsforprojects.com

# Contents

# Tarantula

**The biggest spiders in the world are bigger than your hand.** These tarantulas are sometimes called bird-eating spiders and they really do eat birds, especially baby birds in nests. They also hunt insects, worms and baby rats.

Tarantulas hunt at night. Most look for food on the ground, but some types of tarantula actually live in trees.

The female tarantula keeps watch over her eggs. They are surrounded by a silk shell called a cocoon.

Tarantulas are not poisonous but they have big fangs that they use to bite their prey with.

5

# Wolf spider

**The wolf spider does not make a web like most other spiders.** Instead it chases after victims, like a real wolf would do. It uses its eight big eyes to spot its prey, and runs after it on its eight long legs.

The wolf spider hunts using its eight eyes. Its very large eyes point forwards, for a good view of its prey.

The wolf spider eats any creature it can catch, from a slow slug to a leaping cricket.

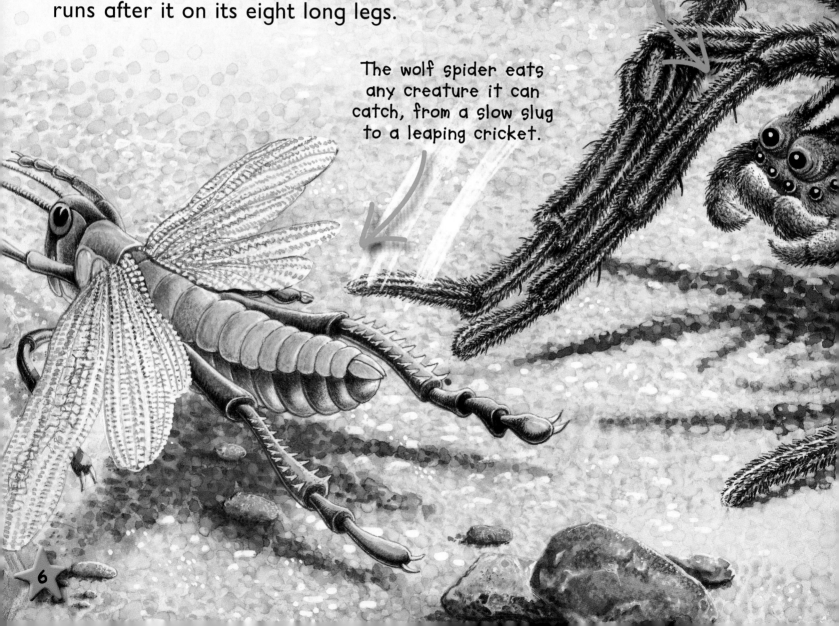

The wolf spider's head and body are quite small, but its legs are long and very powerful.

### Making babies!
The female wolf spider lays eggs and wraps them in a silk case for protection. A few weeks later, the baby spiders hatch.

Wolf spiders sunbathe on pebbles, soil or leaves before they hunt.

# Black widow

**All spiders have a poisonous bite to kill prey or stop it struggling.** Only a few spiders have poison powerful enough to harm a person. The black widow spider may be small but its bite can kill a human. Its close cousin, the redback spider, is just as dangerous.

Only the female has a poisonous bite. She will only bite if she feels threatened, as she can't run away.

The black widow spider is so called because when she has finished mating, the female spider eats the male.

8

## New for old!

Spiders grow by getting rid of, or moulting, their 'skin' — the old body case. There's a new, bigger one underneath.

The female is larger than the male. She has a red mark shaped like an '8' on the underside of her body.

# Crab spider

The crab spider is coloured and shaped to look like part of a flower. Blending into the surroundings like this is called camouflage. Many spiders do this. They may look like leaves, bark, twigs and even bird droppings! Camouflage hides the spider from its prey until it is close enough to pounce.

Just like real crabs at the seaside, crab spiders have wide bodies, and they walk sideways too.

Bees, flies, beetles and ants make a tasty snack for the crab spider.

These spiders keep very still, until their victim is close enough to bite.

## Colourful crabs!

Crab spiders come in many colours and always sit on a flower of the same colour.

# House spider

**House spiders don't go in the bath to get clean.** When they prowl about at night, they may go too near the edge of a bath or sink, and slide in by accident. They can't climb back out because the sides are too steep and slippery. They need help!

House spiders spin untidy-looking webs in corners. The web is triangle-shaped. It is called a cobweb.

House spiders are helpful. They eat flies, mosquitoes and other pests. If you find one in the bath or sink – save it!

**Save a spider!**
Ask a grown up to help you. Put a glass over the spider. Then slide some card under it and lift the card and glass together. Put the spider outside.

The palps feel the way.

The fangs grab and bite prey.

13

# Funnelweb spider

**Most spiders are very shy.** If you go too near, they hide in a dark corner. The funnelweb spider of Australia may do this – or it may rear up, show its big fangs, and get ready to attack. This is very dangerous. The funnelweb is a big, strong spider, and its bite can kill a person.

The funnelweb feeds at night. It feels for its food in the dark with its long front legs.

Silk threads make a funnel shape that leads to the spider's home – a hole under a rock or plant root.

## Spider danger!
You should never put your hands into holes or corners where poisonous spiders live. It is very dangerous.

Prey gets trapped by the silk threads, then the spider kills it with its poisonous bite.

# Spitting spider

**This spider spits a sticky liquid, like glue, from its fangs.** It sprays over its prey like a rope or net. The prey gets tangled up and stuck down. Then the spitting spider moves in, gives a poisonous bite, and begins to feed.

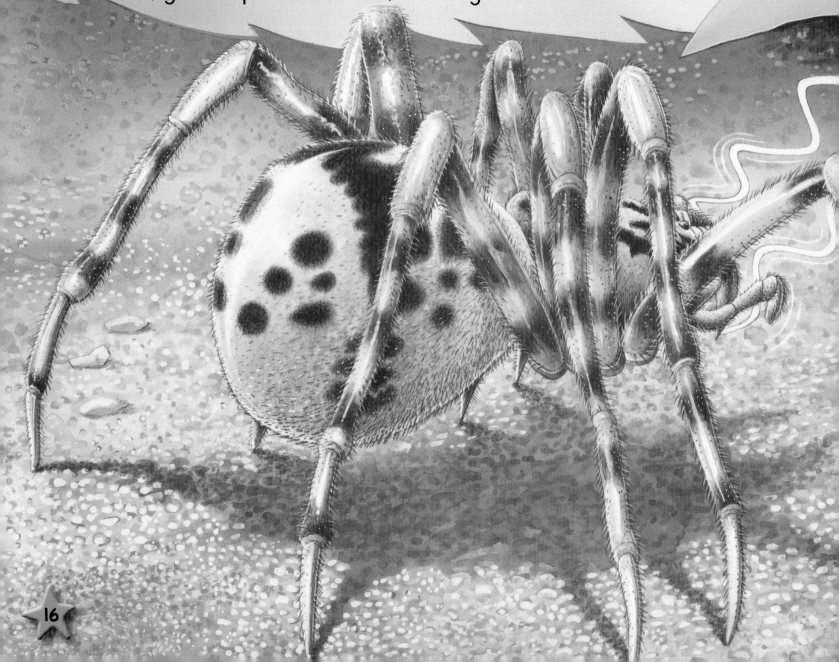

These spiders like to eat tiny insects such as ants, flies and midges.

The spit becomes thick and sticky as soon as it comes out of the spider's fangs.

The spider shakes its head from side to side as it spits. This forms two zig-zag ropes that fall onto the victim and pin it down.

## Spitting distance

The spitting spider can spit three times its own length!

# Raft spider

**The Raft spider sits on a leaf or stone, at the edge of a pond or marsh.** Its front legs dip in the water and can feel the tiny ripples of small creatures moving nearby. The spider dashes across the water, grabs its victim, and races back to land to eat its meal.

Air bubbles get trapped on the spider's hairy body and legs. These help it to float on water.

Raft spiders are big enough to grab small fish, water insects, pond snails, tadpoles and even small frogs.

18

## Fishing for flies!

Fish for flies using a magnet, string and paper clips with paper 'wings' as flies. The 'flies' stick to the magnet if you're quick enough!

The raft spider uses palps, which look like short legs on either side of the fangs, to feel for food.

19

# Orb-web spider

All spiders can make silk threads, but not all spiders make webs from them. The orb-web spider weaves a beautiful web shaped like a wheel. It has strong, straight threads and sticky spiral threads that catch the spider's prey.

Long, straight threads give the web strength. The whole web takes about one hour to build.

## New from old!

The orb-web spider makes a new web each day. First, it eats the old one, to recycle it. This means less new silk has to be made.

If the spider has just eaten, it will wrap up any new prey in silk, and store it to eat later on!

Spiral threads are soft, stretchy and sticky. Flies and moths just can't escape from them.

When a victim gets stuck, the spider feels the threads pull and knows it has caught a meal.

21

# Water spider

**There is only one spider that lives in water.** The water spider breathes air like other spiders. By bringing small air bubbles under the water, this spider uses them to make a bigger bubble. This bubble home provides the spider with air.

The water spider's home is a big bubble or 'air bell'. It eats, rests, and even has its babies there.

In the winter, water spiders do not leave their air bubble. They only come out when it gets warmer.

To catch food, such as tadpoles, water spiders have to poke their legs out of their air bubble.

## Sea spider
The sea spider looks like a spider and lives in the sea. But it is not a real spider, just a close cousin.

# Fun facts

**Tarantula**  When they feel threatened, tarantulas make a purring sound and raise their front legs in defence.

**Wolf spider**  The wolf spider lives on the ground and can run very quickly.

**Black widow**  The male black widow spider is tan and cream in colour.

**Crab spider**  There are around 3000 different types of crab spider in the world.

**House spider**  Male house spiders are smaller than females but they have longer legs.

**Funnelweb spider**  This spider's bite can kill people, but it has no effect on other mammals such as cats and dogs.

**Spitting spider**  The spitting spider lives for a long time, between 2 to 4 years!

**Raft spider**  The female raft spider carries her eggs on her back in a green egg sac.

**Orb-web spider**  Most orb-web spiders are blind or cannot see very well, but they can still tell the difference between day and night.

**Water spider** This spider only comes onto dry land to shed its skin.